THE CONFID

Develop an attitude th

Darren Fisher

with Reji Laberje

Darren Fisher

In The Words Of A Client . . .

Darren is awesome. I've known Darren for about four years and he can really read people. He helps people understand their personal WHYs and how to get to that purpose.

I was one of the first people to use his SPEAR process, when it was just a paper version. After using it for just a quarter, I felt so much more accomplished. I know my plan for each day because I do all my planning the day before and I don't have to think about the next day. I know when I'm OFF TRACK. I know that I'll feel less stressed when I get back on the SPEAR.

Prior to SPEARITY, I was ignoring success and failure, working on auto-pilot, doing, doing, and doing without a plan, always under the gun. Now I feel more productive when I leave and it makes me more productive when I'm home. I use the personal side, too. I feel so much better leaving work and I'm not nervous about coming back into work. I know that I've planned and I'm energized with what I have to get done.

The SPEAR is everything in its place and I'm able to avoid the "got-a-minute" moments throughout the day. I simply add them to my SPEAR. I spend the same amount of time as I did before, but my stress levels are significantly decreased . . . my focus increased.

~Tammi Barrett, Marketing Manager, SWICK Technologies.

This work is based on the experiences of an individual. Every effort has been made to ensure the accuracy of the content.

Quantity order requests can be emailed to:
publishing@rejilaberje.com
Or mailed to:
Reji Laberje Writing And Publishing
Publishing Orders
234 W. Broadway Street
Waukesha, WI 53186

Fisher, Darren
The Confidence Quadrant

Contributing Author: Reji Laberje, Reji Laberje Author Programs
Contributing Editor: Stacy Marie Lewerenz
Interior Design: Reji Laberje
Cover Design: Katie Kimes-Lettau
Photos and Graphics: Stacy Kaat, Katie Kimes-Lettau

ISBN-10: 0692702113
ISBN-13: 978-0692702116
    BISAC Codes:
    BUS046000 Business & Economics/Motivation
    BUS063000 Business & Economics/Strategic Planning
    SEL027000 Self-Help/Personal Growth/Success

Writing and Publishing
www.rejilaberje.com

Darren Fisher

Dedication

In **_"Drive,"_** by Daniel Pink, he tells us that every child in his or her heart is a risk-taker. Somehow, our life experiences influence us to shrink our dreams and spiral into an auto-pilot mindset. We don't have to live that way! People can choose to enjoy life, even when the circumstances within them are not our choices. The Confidence Quadrant™ and SPEARITY™ are about giving people another shot to achieve the big, risk-taking dreams of childhood with their adult-defined purposes.

That's who this book is for.

Specifically, if I don't say it enough, this book is a result of relationship and learning from my mother, Marva. She taught me to embrace flaws and imperfections, while being guided by consistent, unshakeable values. I know if I want to be great, I have to figure out ways to walk the endearing path that she led me on if I'm going to achieve my life purpose. I am not trying to be my mother, but the shortest path to greatness is finding somebody who is greater than you and emulating them.

Marva, I admire you more than I can express in words, but I hope those words I have in this book are a testament to your tenacity and unconditional love and support.

Darren Fisher

Table Of Contents

About This Book

"The Confidence Quadrant" is a practical book. You will be asked to reflect as you work through each chapter. If you can't answer, "What is my takeaway?", then you are not growing. You will learn that if you are not growing, you are shrinking.

The terms, "Confidence Quadrant™," "Auto-Repeater™," "Fearful Doer™," "Overconfident Reciter™," "Confident Enterpriser™," and "Spearity™" are trademarks of Darren Fisher Consulting.

This book is a *Reji Laberje Writing and Publishing* interactive text. In this book, you will find QR codes that will provide insight into what is being shared. Find a free QR scanner for your smart device via a search through your device's app store. Scan the inserted QR codes with your smart device to discover online resources. Further information from the QR codes can be found on the **Electronic Resource Hub (ERH)** for *"The Confidence Quadrant."*

Want to try it out? Visit the ERH through the below QR code and get ready to grow confident and adaptable in order to be your greatest you!

Electronic Resource Hub
"The Confidence Quadrant"
dfisherconsulting.com/the-confidence-quadrant

Darren Fisher

THE CONFIDENCE QUADRANT

I was born to help people pursue greatness. Now that I know this, I've made it my mission to see others realize their potential. Are you pursuing your greatness?

Confidently,

DF

THE "CONFIDENCE QUADRANT" IS BORN

Do your best even when no one is watching, because someone is always watching.

~Marva Bredendick

 I was born in Milwaukee, Wisconsin, in 1971, to a family that already had one son and two daughters (another son came after me). My older brother, Ed, suffered from epileptic seizures. He would never be well enough to care for himself so the tasks of his care came to us as a family. My mom, of course, shouldered the bulk of the responsibility, but helping him during one of his seizures was a task that all family members compassionately undertook.

People might think that growing up with a disabled brother was a disadvantage, but it was not. Our home and normal, everyday activities were actually average to us, but extraordinary measures to give Ed an ordinary life are just what we did; it's all we knew. In hindsight for me, serendipitously, that life conditioned me to keep myself together at those times when life seemed to be falling apart. In Malcolm Gladwell's book, *"David And Goliath,"* Gladwell redefines advantages and disadvantages. He states:

> *A number of the chapters in David and Goliath are about people who turned what seemed like disadvantages into advantages because they refused to be passive in the face of adversity. One of the chapters is about how many dyslexics end up as successful entrepreneurs. I talked to many people like this, and what was fascinating was how many of them said that their success came not in spite of their disability but because of it. Because*

they couldn't read, they forced themselves to learn other things to compensate. You make it through school, if you can't do the thing that schools require of you, by forming alliances with good students, negotiating with teachers, becoming a really good problem solver, learning how to delegate responsibilities, learning how to listen — all the things, in short, that will end up serving you very well in the real world. What all those people had in common, in other words, was a refusal to think of their disability as a disability. They viewed it as an opportunity to learn a new way of doing things. That's the lesson the rest of us can learn.

Identifying our "David Moments" in life is about finding challenges which on their surfaces seem like disadvantages, but—because of the lessons they've taught us—were actually advantages. Due in great part to being raised with my brother, Ed, I don't lose control during unpredictable stressful experiences. To many, a seizing child would create anxiety and fear. For me, it was just part of life and its lessons. I garnered acceptance of adverse circumstances and developed the skills necessary to overcome the fear and anxiety. Adversity is never an excuse to prevent or stifle individual achievement. In my home, I watched my mother juggle the fragile balance between structure and sentiment to keep, not just my brother, but all of us moving forward toward adulthood.

As a teenager, my parents went through a divorce that was emotionally difficult on me. I was a physical late bloomer and that reality had mental and social impacts. Looking back, I realize that I didn't know who I was or what I was trying to do with my life. Even though I attended the top classes in my schools, my confidence was wracked by my emotional and physical maturity.

I was fortunate to recognize that I didn't have the discipline to become whatever it was that I was supposed to become. My sister, Dawn, was in the Air Force. I knew a little about military life and the structure it could provide, so I answered Uncle Sam's call for the next phase of life; I became Airman Darren Fisher. When I went into the Air Force at age eighteen, I was told I might have been chosen to be dorm chief in basic training, but I had such a baby face, that my leaders weren't sure I could merit my brothers' respect. I became chow runner, instead. Chow runners didn't have authority, but had about as frightening of a job as existed within the (in reality) safe and secure walls of Lackland Air Force Base in San Antonio, Texas. We had to go ahead of our unit and "ask permission" to eat on behalf of everyone. We would report to the drill sergeants at the front of the hall and humbly ask before the unit was allowed to pass through the line.

It was essentially the job of all of the trainers to make the chow runners shake in their shined and polished, standard-issue combat boots. The table we reported to was called "the snake pit" and the snakes within it had no problem hissing you out in front of the entire squadron. Lucky for me were two older-and-occasionally-domineering-siblings; they made me tough enough to not be rattled by the rattlers. My trainers had nothing on my sisters, Dawn and Katrina.

As small of a start as that was, the snake pit catalyzed a new confidence. **I started to understand myself.** After Lackland, I trained to become an Attack Control Systems Specialist and, continuing in my military career, was considered cocky. I didn't know I was being brash; I just wanted to be great at everything I did *(confidence without humility, though, is the definition of cocky, but we'll get to that later)*.

At nineteen-years old, in one instance during my Air Force days, I was sent to temporary duty (TDY) in Turkey. It was one of two major deployments I would undertake while I wore the uniform. A plane at the base had been down for three months and the supervisors had a GE engineer on site working the issue prior to my arrival. As a mere Airman, I was about as lowly as they got in terms of respect, but I was sent over by my Tech Sergeant to consult with the engineer and develop a solution. In retrospect, I realized that I'd probably been sent over to "get schooled" and humbled, but I'd done my studying and I knew the fundamentals of troubleshooting. I was open to finding a solution. I didn't know better than to do what I was told at the time, so I offered my solution. There was a wiring issue causing the outage in the plane's systems. I told my supervisors as much after a half a day of diagnostics and reading through the schematics. The engineer argued with me, but—despite his doubts—he tested it and, sure enough, it was the wiring issue I'd identified. The plane was fixed and I was awarded the Air

Force Achievement Medal from the high level, but nothing from my immediate supervisors.

What I thought would be celebrated was, in fact, fuel for envy. A few detractors wanted to pull me down to keep themselves looking better. **Aside from gaining an understanding of myself, I gained a better understanding of people's motivations.**

After my military days, the first time I discussed the business world with my Mom was when I became a teacher. She was a teacher, too, so I knew she could relate. I talked to her about the different ways to build my classroom and have my students become successful. I used to get so frustrated because knowledge would come to me quickly, but it wasn't coming that way for my students in the classroom. I couldn't make things happen for them the way they worked for me.

"I can relate to that," she told me (in reference to the children in my classrooms). "It didn't come easy to me, either. We all process information differently."

What? I had a realization that *my* world wasn't *the* world. I never thought that I was smart. I just figured that— if people did things as I did—they would succeed, too. In my mind, we all processed the same way and I just assumed that all areas where Mom succeeded were by nature; I didn't think she had to take time to process and develop her methods. I learned to copy those people who I thought were better than me and Marva, my mom, was definitely one of those people.

Marva has always been a high achiever who wants to do better. She's a forward thinker, problem solver, and middler in both positive and negative situations. Marva's always been loved by everybody she's touched. In family, friendships, work, and church, her goal was simple: *continuously do whatever she could to put her kids in the best position to succeed.* When it came to achievements, mom would say, "It takes success to make success."

My mother is my friend, my mentor, and my buddy. If I'm feeling down, she's going to bring me up, BUT, if I'm feeling just a little *too* up, she won't hesitate to knock me down a notch (hence the middler moniker)! Marva is tough, but she's also very tender-hearted. To me, she's a genius in her ability to see patterns within people and her surroundings. Mom draws conclusions based on the philosophy or logic that might be behind those patterns. Also, when it comes to diligence, no one will ever outwork Marva. She is a lifelong learner who has, over her lifetime, always been the first one up each day.

After her retirement from teaching, she, along with her brother (my uncle), Hugh, started her own cleaning business. Forever seeking self-improvement and growth, she went back to school to learn new skills in areas as diverse as upholstery and biblical history. She always keeps the latest technology in phones, computers, and programs. Moreover, she doesn't want people to take care of them for her. She wants to be taught *how* so that she can operate the technology on her own. In short, from a desire to teach others, to my love of entrepreneurship, my mom's influence is ever present in my life.

Through my revelatory experiences with my mother, I knew there *was* a way to break through to the learners in the students I had. **I needed to think the way others think.**

One of the things that teaching did for me, though, was to teach *me*—at the administrative level—that, like the Air Force, institutions don't necessarily bring out the best in *people*. Instead, they maintain the *institutions*, themselves, rather than working toward the advancement of the original purpose of the organization's creation.

This organizational evolution (more appropriately denoted as devolution) is not unique. Governments and corporations are no different in their need for self-preservation than an individual's desire to succeed. Most institutions are set up to solve a specific problem: do something, make something, help someone, or meet a need. Eventually, though, the purpose of an organization is to exist despite successfully solving issues. The organizations that adapt and grow from success and failure become something better; they break the mold and become purposeful.

Many schools adapt, too, but some are slower to do so. As with corporations and governments, the bigger schools become, with more and larger moving pieces, the more difficult they are to adopt change, in order to achieve success. Good enough is the mantra if it means the comfort of keeping things as they've always been. I felt that, while teaching, my ability to help people become great was limited by an institution that was trying to maintain itself rather than serve its purpose of educating young people. The traditional teaching career wasn't going to be for me. *I now had some organizational understanding.*

Based on that philosophy of understanding, I moved on to the next phase of my life - entrepreneurship. Using skills I developed during breaks while teaching, I embraced my passion for computer science and attained my MCSE certification. I was able to build DaryDay consulting (named for my daughter, Daryan, and my son, Daylen). My company taught schools and organizations the ins and outs of making technology work for efficiency and other advantages. Entrepreneurship brought more layers to my organizational comprehension, eventually, building my start-up into a half million dollar a year enterprise.

I now had a little understanding of myself, a little understanding of others, a little organizational understanding, and a little understanding of organizational systems. I didn't know it at the time, but I was beginning to breathe life into what would eventually become *"The Confidence Quadrant."*

Although on the path, I was still missing a few pieces to this wholistic creation. I needed to understand the relational and emotional components that would ultimately round out my vision to create a tool that would bring success to anybody, regardless of varying approaches to teaching, learning, and applying.

Enter parenthood!

My son was four years old and he needed a basketball coach. The team asked if I wanted to fill the role. Honestly, I didn't want to do it. I spoke to good ole Mom about it and she told me she thought it would be good for me to coach.

I did and it was the best decision I could have ever made. **That's when I began to learn about the different talents and personalities of people.**

My son was seemed to be born with a ball in his hand. I never had to tell him to pick one up. It appeared to me as if he had this innate talent. On the contrary was my daughter. In her youth, she seemed to be anti-everything—dance, cheerleading, sports, arts. She appeared "less talented" than my son.

Working tirelessly on a daily basis to teach her the fundamentals, eventually my daughter went on to become all-conference softball player.

I remember that, when she was in the 5th grade, Daryan came home and said, "Dad, I got picked in dodge ball before a bunch of the boys because I have one of the best arms."

At the start of her playing days, though, she couldn't consistently hit a wall that was six feet away.

Skills can be developed. Personalities were another issue.

My son could come out of a baseball tournament hitting two for nine and say his take-away was, "I can hit anything! "My daughter could come out of a game she'd won in which she'd performed nine out of ten plays incredibly well and her only remark would be about the one play she'd missed.

My son's and daughter's personalities were a part of who they'd always been –originated from nature. I couldn't change genetic code or nature. What I could do is work with their skills and focus on results to help them tap into what could be developed rather than just rely on what was innate character. **Parenting and coaching with others helped me grow an understanding of combining skill sets with personality types to create success.**

At this time in my life, I felt like I was crushing it! I was a dad, an entrepreneur with a successful business, a son, a husband, and a coach to great kids and athletes. My personal and professional business confidence was high and I believed *'this is what happens when talented people work hard.'*

I can look back today and recognize that I was possibly overconfident . . . probably cocky . . . definitely arrogant. **Life was about to slap me with the emotional piece of my coaching tool.**

I got divorced.

I lost my business.

I let my confidence . . . *disintegrate.*

The reality and effect of divorce and loss still hurts today. Cultural messages would have us believe these things are too commonplace to harbor pain, but ask *anyone* who has actually been through them and you'll get a different story. My whole outlook on life changed. I thought I'd been chasing greatness and that it would "just come" to people who worked hard like I'd been doing, but—in reality—I was living on auto-pilot, not aware of the positives *and* negatives bringing me to that point.

What that point looked like was ugly. I found myself for days at a time only able to eat a couple of grapes here and there. If I tried really hard, I might eat an entire taco from Taco Bell. I withered away. Unable to soundly sleep, I would wake up at all hours of the night to a pillow filled with sweat as I anguished in worry about the life that I seemingly destroyed. I didn't like the life I was living or the person I had become.

I was living in my mother's basement with my two little children. I was thirty years old, and feeling the unbearable weight of failure. In this literal and figurative abyss, I remember being down on my knees in that basement crying out for God to change *me.* I recognized that I didn't have the power to change myself and altering my circumstances without changing me within them wouldn't really make a difference at all. There was no amount of intelligence, gifts, or talents that could have made the difference at that time. In hindsight, I know that God gave me over to my arrogant and egotistical self and, in that hour of desperation, I realized that my "greatness" did not come from my own achievements; it truly comes from my ability to help *others* achieve *their* greatness—it comes from giving , not *to* myself, but *of* myself.

I was frail and broken, but I'd found a purpose.

Every story of success starts from a bottom point. How low that bottom is differs for each person, but it is up to that person to decide in which direction to proceed. On my knees in my mother's basement was my bottom. I needed to find my direction. For me, it was God. It is up to each person to decide what to climb toward. For me, the goal was to move from served to servant by helping others climb toward their goals.

I went back to teaching. I would later recognize the positive gained from going to something familiar, in order to build confidence. Humbled in my approach this time, I began to crush it by meeting my students where they were. This was great on the individual level, but I had the same organizational issues as those I'd faced before and it just wasn't working for me. My younger brother, Bryan, snapped me out of it. "If you were a successful businessman one time, you can do it again," he said.

This was a wise perspective, one with sincere care and compassion. It was easier for him to evaluate me in a non-biased way from the outside looking in, than it was for me to assess myself. I appreciated his words and the encouragement of other close friends and family members who cared about me.

Despite newfound confidence in my direction, I had lost a lot of confidence in my process. **I needed to focus on something greater than me – something that was eternal versus temporary and legacy-related versus day-to-day living.**

When the opportunity arose for me to go back into technology, I seized it and started my own business once again, helping people to solve their technical problems. After reading Simon Sinek's ***"Start With Why,"*** I gained insight in articulating my life's purpose. Sinek teaches that we should gather our stories, articulate our "WHY," refine our "WHY," and take action. I saw that my purpose wasn't about solving a technical problem, it was about solving a leadership problem. That purpose was where I could address greatness. Fundamentally, I believe that if you can take a breath, you're already successful. However, there is always a greater success in you.

> *I wanted to strategically combine my knowledge of confidence, organizational awareness, personality and skill set differences, and relational and emotional understanding to help individuals and organizations achieve a better success in an intentional way.*

This new goal was the impetus behind The Confidence Quadrant. It highlighted the need to develop a tool to help people achieve results with an understanding of how their attitudes would affect their perceptions of successes and failures.

The Confidence Quadrant defines one's Attitude Application – or mental mindset. It ties together the emotional and analytical, so individuals can achieve the logical.

Goals *are* the logical; the plan to achieve a goal is analytical (the SPEAR process is ideal for this step), and emotion is how an individual feels about how things are going while working toward the goal.

The Confidence Quadrant was born.

"What is your takeaway?"

Identify some of your *"David Moments," or,* **disadvantages** that taught you skills to use as **advantages**:

What understandings have you gained about . . .

Yourself:

Others:

Organizations:

Systems:

Personalities:

Skills:

How have emotions played into your successes and failures? Journal about it below:

Take a moment to think about purpose. What stories gathered from your life play into your purpose today?

How would you articulate your purpose today?

What areas of your purpose do you think need refinement?

What action steps can you take to begin a journey toward your purpose?

Failures and Successes are not exclusive to anybody. However, did you ever wonder how two individuals can have the same experience, the same successes, or the same failures, yet takeaway entirely different results?

Confidently,

DF

D<small>ISCOVERING</small> Y<small>OUR</small> A<small>TTITUDE</small> A<small>PPLICATION</small>

Being open to correction means making ourselves vulnerable, and many people are not willing to do that.

~Myles Munroe

We all have attitude tendencies.

The way we approach conflict and compromise, trials and triumphs, and fears and follies is determined by the attitude we apply to toward the different scenarios. We may be born with certain traits that anchor our attitudes, yet attitude may be learned through experience (***developed***).

While you may see some of yourself in parts of each of ***The Confidence Quadrant's*** four ***"Attitude***

Applications," and—more than likely—you will even go through cycles *within* each of the quadrants during your lifetime, odds are you have a **Developed Attitude Application.**

Everyone, by disposition, family of origin, education, experience, and a combination of these areas, has developed an attitude towards success and failure. Intentionally or unintentionally, those attitudes towards success and failure are reinforced as being "good" or "bad".

Consider the following ten questions to discover your own attitude applications and how they affect your personal, professional, and relational lives. Remember that attitude applications are not judgments; rather, they are tools to make you self-aware and better able to manage your situations, relationships, and environments to achieve success in all areas of your life.

Attitude Application Assessment

1 - You are working in outside sales and the company's overall average of successfully closed sales on the product you are tasked with moving is one in every thirty customers. Based on sales calling, alone, how do you feel about your job?

A) Generally frustrated. I know I'm going to hear "no," many times and there's not much I can do about it.

B) Excited. I know exactly how often I'm guaranteed to hear "yes."

C) Overwhelmed. I worry that I won't get enough "yeses."

D) Relatively confident. I understand the challenge and can make a calling plan based on historical sales numbers.

2 - Which of the following would be the most likely phrase those close to you would use to describe you?

A) He/she is "very hard on himself/herself."

B) He/she is "extremely competitive."

C) He/she is a "perfectionist."

D) He/she is a "self-made man/woman."

3   - You are learning to manipulate a graphic in a new computer program, and after more than a dozen attempts at making the picture look as it should, you are unsuccessful. What is the most likely thing you would do next based on the following choices?

A) Keep trying even though I probably won't be able to figure it out.

B) Skip it. There must be something wrong with the program.

C) Spend hours in the community forums and on YouTube tutorials learning about and practicing different things to try to become an expert at the program.

D) Read the "Help" section of the program and, if there is no answer, ask colleagues what has and has not worked for them until I find a solution.

4   - Which of the following would be a great life motto?

A)   Live in the moment!

B)   Look out for number one.

C)   Hard work pays off.

D)   Born winner!

5   - You're tasked with being on the committee for the fundraiser of your child's sport organization. What role would you prefer?

A) None. These fundraisers rarely make a difference.

B) Finding quality donations. You need the right means to get the job done.

C) Worker bee. Just tell you what to do and you'll get it done.

D) Committee Chair. You prefer to lead others for the bigger picture.

6   - How would you describe the way in which you have come by successes in your lifetime?

A) I had successes in most life areas when I was young, but began to struggle the older I became.

B) Early success came easy for me across many different life areas and skill sets.

C) I've had to work for every single success I've achieved in every area of my life

D) I'm not successful in all areas and I work in the areas where I am successful.

7 - When you participated in sports or competitive organizations in your *youth*, which of the following scenarios applied most often to you?

A) I wasn't very competitive, but it wasn't that important to me.

B) I was a great competitor, but wasn't really appreciated enough to get used as much as I should have been.

C) I was a pretty good competitor, but it didn't come naturally; I was known for being a dedicated, hard worker.

D) I did well enough. I didn't work as hard as some of the other players, but I did spend time working on the things that needed improvement.

8 - One of your entry-level, lower wage employees shows up to work late and unprepared for the third time. How do you confront him or her?

A) It's hard to find quality people for entry level jobs. I say nothing because I know it won't really make a difference and I don't have time to replace him/her.

B) When he/she comes into my office, I give him/her the cold shoulder. He/she knows I don't appreciate the behavior.

C) I call him/her into my office right away, shut the door, and fire him/her. I've had enough. I'd be better just doing his/her work on my own.

D) It would depend on the employee's situation and personality, but I would need to spend some time coming up with an appropriate plan.

9 - At a party, you have:

A) Many people to talk to, but few true friends.

B) A blast! I'm the last to leave.

C) An uncomfortable feeling, but nobody knows it. I'm friendly with everybody.

D) A plan about who I should talk to about what.

10 - In a fearful situation, your natural instinct is:

A) FREEZE! I don't know how to deal.

B) FLIGHT! I'm out of there.

C) FIGHT! It's the only way out of the trouble.

D) FORETHOUGHT! I need to assess the situation before deciding whether I should freeze, fight, or take flight.

Total up your answers:

>Number of A Answers-_____
>
>Number of B Answers-_____
>
>Number of C Answers-_____
>
>Number of D Answers-_____

Your *Attitude Application* is based on the letter with the largest number of associated answers and your *Developed Attitude Application* is based on the letter with the second highest number of associated answers.

If you answered mostly A, your Attitude Application is **Auto-Repeater**.

If you answered mostly B, your Attitude Application is **Overconfident Reciter**

If you answered mostly C, your Attitude Application is **Fearful Doer.**

If you answered mostly D, your Attitude Application is **Confident Enterpriser**.

Awareness of your Attitude Application is only the first step in working toward success. Understanding your application and how it plays out in your life is where the real work of The Confidence Quadrant begins.

"What is your takeaway?"

How would you describe your attitude toward success?

How would you describe your attitude toward failure?

Based on the questions in the Attitude Application Assessment and your answers to them, what specific self-awareness do you expect to discover about your personal and professional attitude?

What are you hoping to gain from "The Confidence Quadrant?" Journal about it below:

Greatness by nature is counter-cultural. We all want "better," but we want it without having to actually change what we're doing. True greatness comes from being better . . . intentionally.

Confidently,

DF

WHAT ARE SUCCESS AND FAILURE, REALLY, AND WHY DO THEY MATTER?

The greatest day in your life and mine is when we take total responsibility for our attitudes. That's the day we truly grow up.

~John C. Maxwell

As we start digging into success, it's important to define it, as well as a few other terms that we'll be visiting throughout the learning ahead. Success can be defined a number of ways including:

- From Dictionary.com, the favorable or prosperous termination of attempts or endeavors;

- ℰ According to Merriam Webster, the fact of getting or achieving wealth, respect, or fame;
- ℰ And—if you go by way of the Oxford English Dictionary—the accomplishment of an aim or purpose.

The problem with definition is its inherent subjectivity. At the end of the day, for instance, what I may call "achieving wealth," might not be the same as what a Saudi Prince calls "achieving wealth." Even what I consider prosperity or respect may vary greatly from the idea another person has for those words. Still others may think achieving certain aims or purposes aren't even worthy of the term "success."

What if, instead, **we look at success as "a *perceived* favorable or desirable result that continues the momentum of a trajectory toward a goal"?** PERCEIVED is the key word. If you are to achieve success, you must perceive what success means . . . *TO YOU.*

Here are a few other definitions that we will use when we reflect on the following words throughout The Confidence Quadrant.

Action – Actual emotional, intellectual, spiritual, or physical tasks that have been, are, or will be completed.

Adaptability – The ability to change after a result of failure and based on the understanding that a repeated action would get a different result.

Attention – Sensory observation and purposeful focus given to a result.

Attitude Application – The creative marrying of failing and succeeding results, with one's emotional perception of those results, in a unified mindset that can be used to approach personal and professional goals.

Better – Intentional, positive growth.

Confidence *(SELF Confidence)* – A feeling of success that comes from within, but is not necessarily backed up by measurable actions and results; your belief that success can be repeated based on the observations from either the past successful results.

Confidence *(TRUE Confidence)*–A feeling of success that is backed up, not just by a personal emotion, but also by measurable action.

Enterpriser – A willing risk-taker who embraces success and failure for constant improvement.

Favorable – Positive movement in *the direction of* (not necessarily *at the finish line of*) the target

Focus – Special importance or habitual attention given to results.

Greatness – Working *toward* your purpose by being better in an intentional way.

Grow – Progressive development of an area in your life.

Habitual – Something that becomes automatic, routine, natural, and ingrained.

Ignore – Refusal to take notice of or acknowledge; to disregard intentionally.

Importance – Value and purpose assigned to the result to which you are working.

Intentional –Making a plan, finding a system that tracks a plan and keeping to the plan in a measured way.

Perceived – Your own subjective perspective in reflecting on an outcome.

Purpose – Different for everybody, this is a well-defined "WHY" to guide us in our actions.

Refusal – A conscious decision or subconscious habit of determining that the result was not something from which you could gain confidence or adaptability (see below).

Results – Any past event is a result, success or fail. There is always a success or failure every single time. The outcome is the result.

Shrink –The reality of what happens when something is not growing. Nothing is constant; if we are not growing into our purpose, we are shrinking from it.

Special– Set aside and intentional emphasis or attention given to something or someone.

Takeaway – An introspective look and intentional noting of what you have gained intellectually, emotionally, or spiritually after reading, seeing, hearing, learning, or experiencing something.

For decades, society has been slowly fading out our usage of the word "FAIL." Even our school systems have, for the most part, eliminated letter systems that dare to indicate somebody's precious child has failed as shown by the "F" at the top of a test or paper. We have ingrained in us, on a cultural level, professional level, personal level, emotional level, mental level, and—in many cases—even a spiritual level, that "FAIL" is the real taboo.

The avoidance of the word failure is the product of a society that is so affluent it is able to remove any negative or hurtful denotation, even when it's the one thing that allowed a person to become great in the first place. Previous generations embraced failure because on a personal and a societal level failure was used to intentionally grow better. Today, in a world where conveniences reign, we alter reality and pretend that failure doesn't even exist. Like so much of our language, we have just changed the word.

Coaches avoid the term. Parents tell children to ignore it. Even leaders of companies are wary of the word, "FAIL." How many times have you been in a meeting or conversation in any of these scenarios when you've heard *'well, I wouldn't say failure, but opportunity.'*? This is one of many similar variations that shame, shun, and shadow the word "FAIL" out of existence? Will "FAILURE" become a vocabulary word that children fifty years from now have to look up when they read *"classic"* literature pieces that came out in the 1900s?

Even when we do learn about failure, it's often through the lens of ignoring its usefulness. I think Einstein said it best where that method is concerned:

"Insanity: Doing the same thing over and over again and expecting different results."

All of this denial of failure has surely led to a problem-free existence, though, right? We have no troubles, everybody is prosperous, and you don't know a single soul who isn't living his or her dream, right? Or maybe not. Maybe, in reality, failure is the twenty-first century's elephant in the room. Not addressing it or including it doesn't make it go away. We run into it; it's noisy at times; it blocks our way to the things we need to reach; it's uncomfortable; and, denying its existence won't prevent it from stinking up our lives.

Looking at the ugly word, objectively, we can determine a few accepted definitions:

- From Dictionary.com, an act or instance of failing or proving unsuccessful;
- According to Merriam Webster, omission of occurrence or performance; specifically expected action

    Ⓔ And—if you go by way of the Oxford English
    Dictionary—lack of success

Contrarily, success is idolized and idealized. Everybody wants to be the "self-made man or woman" without any regard for the people who sacrificed before him or her, the people currently sacrificing or the opportunities provided to him or her. Success is seen as something that some people just have, and others don't. Or, it's treated as a matter of luck, achievable by those who have had all the breaks given to them. Success is for the rich. The beautiful. The elite. And those who earn it, but usually at the expense of a loss (because we dare not say fail) in some other area of their lives.

Furthermore, success is something that we assume has its own momentum; once it starts happening for a person, it will keep happening forever. *'He/she doesn't know how to fail!'* is an expression most of us have heard said about some high achiever in our lives. This is as dangerous as the elephant in the room.

If **Success** is **"a *perceived* favorable or desirable result that continues the momentum of a trajectory toward a goal,"** then **Failure**, by contrast, must mean, **"*perceived* falling short of a result that stops or reverses the momentum of a trajectory toward a goal."**

Unlike the ignorance of failure or the defaulted expectation of success, The Confidence Quadrant embraces both results to help build repeatable, sustainable processes to keep you tracking toward your personal and professional goals.

The goal of The Confidence Quadrant is to teach how to:

1 – Continue *repeating* the same actions that led to successes to GROW CONFIDENCE.

2 – Avoid *repeating* the same actions that led to failures to GROW ADAPTABILITY.

These two steps, applied *intentionally*, will lead toward a Developed Attitude Application of Confident Enterpriser – or, a courageous, flexible attitude to face every goal.

In addition, you will learn about tools that take goals beyond SMART with a tracking process and system that can turn constant and consistent development into a habitual, actionable part of your life.

One's attitude towards success and failure determines everything.

- Those who focus on success will grow confidence.
- Those who ignore success will shrink confidence.
- Those who focus on failure will grow adaptability.
- Those who ignore failure will shrink adaptability.

It's that simple.

Everyone needs more confidence in order to *crush it* in life and pursue greatness. We also need adaptability to help us when we meet with the inevitable: change. Confidence and adaptability are attitudes that can be developed over time. Just because our family history, parents, school, or work environment influence our attitudes, doesn't mean we're stuck with them. By changing the way we look at our experiences, the twin results of success AND failure, we can live our lives in **The Confidence Quadrant**.

"What is your takeaway?"

Rethinking definitions: Make a list of the words you need to rethink in your life, either from those shared in the chapter you've just finished, or those that came to mind as you began the work of The Confidence Quadrant.

Our environments help to shape more than just our Developed Attitude Applications. They are also vital to our acceptance of words and definitions. Journal about your own experiences and influences and how they've helped shape your definitions.

I'd much rather see a kid swing at a ball ten feet over his head, than watch him look at a third strike. It's easier to adjust to the strike zone after a swing and a miss.

Confidently,

DF

THE AUTO REPEATER™

Don't fake it till you make it. Fake it till you become it.

~Amy Cuddy

In Kindergarten, Angela's parents heard from her teacher that their daughter was lazy. She did great in school because it came easy to her, but she didn't have to really work for it . . . so she didn't. As she got older, though, she struggled. She assumed that because she had been successful in the past she would simply continue to be so. She wasn't willing to work harder when the work *became* harder.

As Angela continued in elementary school, she set goals, but disregarded them carelessly without further review, or—at best—moved the goalposts, in denial of the fact that she had failed at reaching the benchmark. Her attitude in activities and friendships mirrored that of school. In her friendships, there was turmoil. She had no confidence to build lasting, trusting relationships. If a person came back into her life, it was without her having worked for it, and therefore, her connections were more like associations than friendships. In her activities, she would attempt the endeavor, but if it didn't work immediately, she would walk away from it with an attitude of indifference.

Angela found love in those younger and older than her, but not often among her peers.

There was a time she was depressed in middle school. She cried and didn't see a purpose. She wasn't connected. If you aren't seeing successes, there isn't hope. You don't have the ability to change because you believe in inevitability.

The Risk of Spiraling

In this perceived state of inevitability, one can start thinking: 'Success isn't possible,' 'Defeat is external.' It can become easy to project doom and give up. Each of us spirals at times in our lives, and it's necessary to pull out for obvious reasons of mental well-being. There are few things worse than the feeling of permanent, inevitable failure. It's one thing to fail; it's another thing to believe it's going to happen, and keep happening forever.

In this state—a perception of impossible success-- depression is a probable outcome. SPIRALING, or falling into hopelessness and depression based on perceived inevitable failure, is something common to the "Angelas" of the world. Out of the four Confidence Quadrants, she would be the most likely to spiral.

Angela had difficulty seeing success or failure in life, so she tended to live in the moment (or, at least perceived this attitude in herself). When success happened, she dismissed it as not very important or difficult. When failure occurred, there was remorse in the moment, but it was short-lived. After the initial pain was gone, so was the need to adapt.

Angela's attitude is that of a typical Auto Repeater.

The Auto Repeater is someone who ignores success *and* ignores failure. The indifference of the Auto Repeater is generally due to the belief that a failed history will only produce a failed future so "why even try?" This give-up mentality leads to living in constant fear of failure.

We all know, and at times have been, an Auto Repeater. Consider what this Attitude Application might look like in some of the following people in our lives:

Athlete:

He or she doesn't want the ball and doesn't want to practice to be good if he or she does get the ball.

Entrepreneur:

He or she had some setbacks and now is in retreat/survival-mode; the person doesn't want to do anything differently, but is not sure what to do next.

Service Person, Volunteer, or Cause-worker:

This person simply doesn't want to do it, anymore! He or she doesn't feel like a difference is being made.

Parent:

He or she wants to go on vacation and never come back. The parent might check out, wanting to live for himself or herself, rather than be a parent at all.

Professional:

He or she experiences sleeplessness over a loss of purpose and not feeling like he or she could make a difference.

Ways we can all fall into Auto Repeater mode:

If you think about times in your life when you've felt helpless or hopeless, you know that there are ways all of us can fall into Auto Repeater mode. It doesn't mean that we have that as an Attitude Application, but we may develop it at certain times in our lives.

Especially to the Auto Repeater, I say, "FEAR NOT!" First, there are some great traits possessed by Auto Repeaters, and second-of-all, there are ways to break out of the cycle of inevitability being perceived.

Goals

- *Wants to be successful but quits easily*
- *Doesn't really know what she wants to do many times*
- *Goes are set and discarded with regularity*

Character Traits

- *Highly forgetful*
- *Hard on self*
- *Changes the goal, rather than the means to achieve it*

Endearing Qualities

- *Very sweet*
- *Loved by diverse group of individuals*

Connection to the Masses

- *Depression can be a probable outcome*

While an Auto Repeater may feel like he or she is *living* in the moment, the reality is that Auto Repeaters are merely *surviving* in the moment. With focus on neither success (to build confidence) nor failure (to build adaptability); the Auto Repeater must be very intentional about desiring a better perception and outcome. The greatest upside for Auto Repeaters is that they can see the fastest results from just a few simple cycle breakers.

Awareness is the first step toward using The Confidence Quadrant. Look back at the Attitude Application assessment and review all of the "A" answers. Remember that the assessment is not a judgment; it is simply a tool for understanding one's self. Awareness goes beyond just knowing. It means we must both have knowledge and *accept* the implications of that knowledge.

As difficult as it may be to do so, if you see yourself as an Auto Repeater, write below, _"I am aware that my Attitude Application is Auto Repeater."_

Now that you have awareness piece tackled, it's time to work your way toward growing your confidence and your adaptability. For an Auto Repeater, this is a simple two-step process.

1. Write down three daily successes. Start today. Write some simple successes, here:

2. Make daily goal lists including the first goal as "COMPLETE A TO-DO LIST." Try a three-step checklist, here:

Finding successes for an Auto Repeater can be hard. Consider some of the many things that you might take for granted –

- ☜ I made the bed.
- ☜ I went to work.
- ☜ I am working on The Confidence Quadrant right now!

The Auto Repeater is in the lower quadrant of The Confidence Quadrant, opposite the ultimate goal of The Confident Enterpriser, meaning he or she has to move out quickly. The action steps for an Auto Repeater are all about building confidence. From the place of confidence, one can work toward trying new tasks and achieving greatness. While the Auto Repeater also needs to focus on failures, it's easier to get him or her there from one of the outer quadrants. By creating exercises that focus on failure, for a person that does not yet have the skill of adaptation, there is a risk that the Auto Repeater will only have the perception of hopelessness confirmed.

One of the first things people tend to say to somebody who isn't achieving success on a goal is, *'You need to work harder.'* This makes about as much sense as Einstein's insanity definition. Just working harder means you're going to get the same result faster. Instead, you need to work differently. That will BE harder.

Connect with a PLAN for goals. It's about the things that can be done to prepare for a goal. Put those action steps on the To-Do lists. Then – CHECK THEM OFF! Checks on a list are confidence and confidence is the first key to achieving greatness!

"What is your takeaway?"

While your daily to-do lists are likely to be necessary tasking toward goals, consider the daily successes that you may take for granted each day. What are those things for which you can already gain confidence?

Get honest with yourself. Journal about a time that you were depressed or spiraling toward depression. If you look back at that time of your life objectively, can you spot the successes?

Living in fear is basically dying over and over again, which is obviously no way to live.

Confidently,

DF

THE FEARFUL DOER™

*The greatest mistake we make is living
in constant fear that we will make one.*

~John C. Maxwell

Lisa has worked her proverbial tail off to earn her success. She is an over-achiever who believes that the only way to success is to put in more hours, more stress, more money, more effort, more energy, more talent, more, more, more, more, More, MORE, *MORE!* Putting the finish line before most other needs, Lisa will sacrifice whatever it takes to be sure she reaches a goal.

Lisa has always succeeded, beginning with doing well in school and always loved by people in her life. From the outside, people look admirably to Lisa, perhaps not having the realization that, while she looks like she's *crushing it*, whatever "it" is, is probably crushing her.

If you know a Lisa, then you probably know a Fearful Doer.

The Fearful Doer is someone who ignores success *and* focuses on failure. Lisa, In fact, is *keenly aware* of failure. This is what drives her to accomplish great things. Fail...adapt...succeed. Her great results are a testament to this success pattern. Few will argue that it is "working", but at what cost?

Because Lisa ignores her successes, she lacks confidence to believe that those successes will happen again. When she achieves success, she rationalizes it away as something easy or unimportant. On the other hand, when Lisa fails, she **IR**rationalizes that she expected as much, probably as part of her own doing.

The Risk of Spiraling

Fearful Doers are highly prone to spiraling because they, out of all of the Attitude Applications of the Confidence Quadrant, emphasize a focus on failures. Keeping with the pace of a Fearful Doer means that an individual may not believe he or she has the energy to change and adapt saying, *'forget it.'* This is a relational quadrant to live in. As an entrepreneur, one may lose clients and see revenue fall. The Fearful Doer can forget how success began with and can let fear grasp hold.

Many of us have been Lisa at one time or another in our lives. We just don't want to fail again; unfortunately, the failure is not realizing that there have been successes along the way. This is what a Fearful Doer might look like in some of the following people:

Athlete:

These are the better players on the team described as gritty, hard-working, smart, heady players.

Entrepreneur:

This is a conservative leader. He or she has a solid book of business grown in the exact same way; it works and he or she doesn't want to change. Second generation owners are often Fearful Doers. A dad or mom built the company and the entrepreneur may not want to mess up what's been done.

Service Person, Volunteer, or Cause-worker:

These are the worker bees. Just tell them what to do and they'll get it done. They aren't typically the leaders, but they are great doers!

Parent:

Typically, they are the helicopter parents, fighting their children's fights and even doing their homework. These parents operate more in paranoid mode than in protective mode.

Professional:

This person is going to produce the best work; however, it will be all over the place. The work may be last minute and often leaves the professional feeling overwhelmed. The Fearful Doer operates under super stress.

Ways we can all fall into Fearful Doer mode:

When we find ourselves in a place where our failures become so painful that it becomes difficult to focus on our successes, we are in Fearful Doer mode.

Goals

- *Wants to be the best*
- *Constantly rising within the organization*

Character Traits

- *Very hard on self*
- *Guilt-driven*
- *Perfectionist*
- *Moves the goal posts*

Endearing Qualities

- *Sweet person*
- *Liked by everyone*

Connection to the Masses

- *Many of us have been Lisa at one time or another in our lives. We just don't want to fail again;*

unfortunately, the failure is not realizing that there have been successes along the way

Lisa's attitude is the prototypical Fearful Doer. Due to the focus on failure, Fearful Doers usually avoid new projects, work really hard to become successful, and tend to be one of the highest performers on the team. The problem is that they are miserable before, during, and after an accomplishment. Because they ignore their successes, they have difficulty coming up with any positives, resulting in working harder but not necessarily better. Eventually . . . *they run out of energy.*

Awareness is the first step toward using The Confidence Quadrant. Look back at the Attitude Application assessment and review all of the "C" answers. Remember that the assessment is not a judgment; it is simply a tool for understanding one's self. Awareness goes beyond just knowing. It means we must both have knowledge and *accept* the implications of that knowledge.

As difficult as it may be to do so, if you see yourself as a Fearful Doer, write below, _"I am aware that my Attitude Application is Fearful Doer."_

Darren Fisher

1. Find somebody to help you see the successes you have accomplished— even when you don't believe them to be successes. Name some possible partners for this step:

2. WITH the helpful person, write some successes down. Everybody should write successes, but a Fearful Doer may actually need help to do so.

"What is your takeaway?"

Write down the repeatable process of at least one success. It could be as simple as arriving to work on time, noting the time you left, the route you took, where you parked, etc.

Get honest with yourself. Journal about a time that was filled with stress that might have been less overwhelming with a change in attitude,

Humble pie should really be called humble salad. You need to eat it because it's good for you, but the truth is you'd rather avoid it if possible. I love pie, but salad....

Confidently,

DF

THE OVERCONFIDENT RECITER ™

Learning is not compulsory . . . neither is survival.

~W. Edwards Deming

*M*ichael knew success early and easily across a large spectrum of challenges. He has had positive results in academics, sports, music, and friendships. As a natural extrovert, Michael tends to be the life of the party and he owns every room he enters. People love to be around people like Michael.

Michael focuses on his successes and ignores his failures. He is the epitome of an Overconfident Reciter.

The Risk of Spiraling

When an Overconfident Reciter changes quadrants, it's a difficult place to live. They can become addictive or obsessive, seeking new vices or consuming passions. Most Overconfident Reciters don't really spiral at all. They go into a tailspin.

We've all seen Michaels in our lives; you may even be a Michael. They are professionals and high achievers who make the news after falling far and fast. They are the athletes who went from the tops of their games to not being able to succeed at the games' most basic skills after a single undeniable failure. The world's Michaels have a blind spot to failure and when the blinders are taken off, they're devastated.

Athlete:

They believe they're the best, but they don't get as much playing time or notoriety as they think they should.

Entrepreneur:

Their lack of success is blamed on excuses: "It's the economy." "It's the client." "It's NOT the product or service."

Service Person, Volunteer, or Cause-worker:

They recognize that there are people who are suffering and they could help, but they don't have the tools to do it; so they may not work toward the cause at all. If they don't feel needed and praised, you lose them.

Parent:

When they realize that they don't have the influence you thought they did, they are shocked. They respond in surprise when their children exemplify behaviors that they never thought "THEIR KIDS" would do.

Professional:

He or she typically gets lower evaluations than he or she thinks are deserved. As professionals, Overconfident Reciters feel overlooked for rewards or promotions.

Ways we can all fall into Overconfident Reciter mode:

In a word: ARROGANCE. Or, to go back to my Air Force days, maybe you prefer the word, "cocky." In short, ego is the enemy that can trap a person in the Overconfident Reciter quadrant. A lack of humiliation, gratitude, and desire for personal improvement can earn somebody the Overconfident Reciter title. Fast success should be celebrated, but it's important to keep achievements in perspective. The goals of an Overconfident Reciter are admirable, but there are negative traits that can overshadow an Overconfident Reciter's endearing qualities.

Goals

- *Wants to be the best*

Character Traits

- *Blames others when things don't go right*
- *Gets satisfaction from beating lesser opponents*
- *Never sees himself as the problem*

Endearing Qualities

- *Great with people*
- *Loved by people*
- *Lights up a room*

Connection to the Masses

⌕ *Everyone loves the confident person, until they lose confidence. At that point, things change in a hurry. For anyone who's lost their confidence, we can relate to the tailspin effect that can occur with an Overconfident Reciter.*

Dealing with Overconfident Reciters requires a directional perspective. Remember, in helping an Auto Repeater or a Fearful Doer, you have to be a cheerleader, discovering and recording successes that require focus! If I'm an Overconfident Reciter, I may be failing and not even recognizing the failures. I need to recognize it in order to let it drive change. Failure leads to adaptability . . . to change.

What you don't want to do, though, is to lose track of successes when learning to focus on failures. It's important to keep doing the thing you're good at! Keep focusing on success; just bring humility alongside that focus to discover where failures might be hidden.

Awareness is the first step toward using The Confidence Quadrant. Look back at the Attitude Application assessment and review all of the "B" answers. Remember that the assessment is not a judgment; it is simply a tool for understanding one's self. Awareness goes beyond just knowing. It means we must both have knowledge and *accept* the implications of that knowledge.

As difficult as it may be to do so, if you see yourself as an Overconfident Reciter, write below, *"I am aware that my Attitude Application is Overconfident Reciter."*

I'm guessing that there aren't many Michaels reading this book. Working through The Confidence Quadrant requires a degree of awareness and introspection. As an Overconfident Reciter, blinded to failure by success, why would change be sought? There is a line that is crossed when one steps into Michael's quadrant . . . that of an Overconfident Reciter. It's confidence without humility; it's pomposity and arrogance. It's cocky. The potential exists for one who is focusing entirely on success and ignoring failures to lose that "loved by people" quality and drop into a tailspin.

If your assessment had you as an Overconfident Reciter and you picked up this book to seek awareness and potential for development, *congratulations*! You are more than likely already moving out of the Overconfident Reciter quadrant. You are bringing humility and introspection into your life.

1. With a humbled new approach to your attitude application, take a bold step and write down three areas in which you know you could grow.

2. Think outside of yourself. Write down a
   list of people who have different gifts and
   talents than you and who are able to help
   you to achieve success.

The Overconfident Reciter is someone who focuses on successes but ignores failures. They are generally happy go lucky and can find the positive in everything they do (even in the face of repeated failure). Why change if everything is working great? The Overconfident Reciter refuses to see faults in his or her own shortcomings but can identify every other reason why there are failings.

The risk of an Overconfident Reciter is disillusionment and disconnection from reality and real relationships. This could lead, not just into a spiral, but a tailspin. An Overconfident Reciter needs to learn how to objectively evaluate failure without funneling down to the Auto Repeater quadrant.

"What is your takeaway?"

Fight the tailspin. It's important not to lose the ability to focus on success. Write down three things that you feel help you toward success.

Now it's time to get introspective . . . and humble. Pick one of your successes from your takeaway and journal about the factors that helped that success along and had nothing to do with you. What people, systems, foundation, etc. were helpful to you achieving greatness?

Common sense is a myth based on an egocentric viewpoint; it's holding somebody else accountable for learning from one's own experiences.

Confidently,

DF

COOKING UP SUCCESS

*You can easily judge the character of a
man by how he treats those who can do
nothing for him.*

~Simon Sinek

*I*magine a scenario . . .

When Daniel walks into his office on an average work day, he says, "Hello," to the office administrative assistant, Angela. She's reliable, shows up on time, and does exactly what is on her list to be done. While it's nice to have Angela in the office, there is a lot of untapped potential that Daniel suspects will remain that way. Angela is content doing what she's told, but doesn't usually go above and beyond.

Daniel passes by his Human Resources department where Lisa is, as always, diligently working away at a stack of paperwork, ensuring every "i" is dotted and "t" is crossed. Lisa is surrounded by the required posters: Equal Employment Opportunity, Sexual Harassment Policy, Social Media Usage Rules, and the most recent communiqué on proper formatting of emails. Lisa recently applied for a position in accounting and Daniel thinks it would be a good fit because of the special attention she gives to detail.

In Daniel's sales department, all that remains is Michael. At one time, Angela tried her hand at sales, working the metrics of calls, but not making much progress. As a small company, Lisa did sales at one time, too. Her calls were random and, after some major losses, she stopped making calls and started just doing, doing, doing a number of other, less stressful tasks that didn't really result in closed sales. She didn't have the confidence to pick up the phone and settled instead for emails and social media to do the work for her. Nobody could deny how busy Lisa was, but she was just faking it; the results weren't there.

Michael came into the sales department strong, just a month ago. He began to crush it from the start and has ridden those wins to present day. If Michael has a bad week, he's able to pick the phone back up because he remembers the great week he had last month. Unfortunately, after two bad weeks, then three, or even four, Michael still looks back at the great week he had when he began in sales. In reality, his closings have stagnated. In fact, if he turned in his reports, Michael's sales are more than likely falling. He keeps calling, though, so Daniel's not too concerned just yet.

As Daniel looks at his office, he sees a lot of great things, but he knows that this team could do more. What if Angela realized the power of her reliability and how much of a success that is for the company? How could that change her motivation and her willingness to innovate? What if Lisa was able to take her eyes off of her losses long enough to see her wins? Would she feel less inclined to surround herself with rules and more inclined to surround herself with goals? And if Michael saw success as continuous growth rather than past achievements, could he start to have wins with increasing regularity?

Angela was an indifferent worker, while Lisa and Michael were both on autopilot, with Lisa defaulting to busy work and Michael living out Einstein's definition of insanity – not making continuous changes despite the reality that he is no longer attaining his sales goals. When the *whole* team is not working intentionally, the *whole* team is working on autopilot. How could he wake up the passion in his team to drive toward greatness?

The next week, Daniel invited the entire team to his home for pizza and a training exercise. Much to the team's surprise, when they arrived, Daniel's countertop was filled with pizza dough, sauces, spices, cheese, and toppings. One pizza was already put together.

"Michael," Daniel said, "Could you please put the finished pizza in the oven? It's already preheated. I set the timer, so you can just hit start."

While Michael's pizza was cooking, Daniel told Lisa to make a pizza with the ingredients in front of her . . . ALL of the ingredients.

"All at once?" Lisa asked, looking at the countertop cluttered with massive quantities of food. "On one pizza?"

"Everything you need is there," Daniel said.

Lisa then asked about the time and the temperature, making sure to write it down.

"And Angela, let's wait for Michael's pizza to finish.

Michael, Angela, and Daniel sat at the kitchen table while Lisa diligently rolled out the pizza crust; there wasn't much left, so she had to stretch it and patch it, working hard until it was big enough to cover the pizza pan. It was thin in some areas, but at least it was done. She poured on the sauce, way too much, mind you. She dumped the entire bag of cheese on top of the pizza. Some of it squished into the over-abundance of sauce. Then, she piled on the ingredients before her: garlic (all six cloves), pepperoni, sausage, olives, onions, mushrooms, pineapple, and even anchovies. She held her breath while placing those.

By the time Lisa had finished, the timer was going off for Michael's pizza.

"Go ahead and take your pizza out, Michael," Daniel said. "And, Lisa, you can put yours in."

Michael pulled out his pizza and, with Daniel's direction, began to cut it. Before he had even finished, the oven began to smoke. Sauce from Lisa's pizza spilled all over the bottom of the stove. As it dripped down, cheese and toppings fell, as well. The smoke detector began to blare as the air filled with a garlic-scented smoke.

Daniel quietly walked to the oven, turned it off, and pulled out the sloppy, yet uncooked mess that was Lisa's pizza. He turned off the smoke alarm and began to cut Lisa's pizza. Then, he served it up to Angela.

Needless to say, she didn't wish to eat it and the entire team was left very confused.

"Do I have to have more than one slice?" Angela asked.

"I could have Lisa make another one." said Daniel.

"Ha!" Lisa laughed at herself. "Well, obviously, I can't cook."

"Really?" asked Daniel, "and you know that from this one little training exercise?"

"What training exercise? We're just making pizza," Michael jumped in. "Mine looks great!"

Daniel smiled. His Auto Repeater, Fearful Doer, and Overconfident Reciter had all revealed their Attitude Applications.

"Let's clear the smoke," Daniel said, as he opened a window, and he also cleared away the mess that was Lisa's pizza. Placing Michael's pizza in the middle of the table, Daniel explained what their training had been all about:

"Angela, you were willing to eat a pizza that was clearly inedible. It was uncooked, covered in ingredients you didn't care for, and a mess. But, you just assumed that was your only choice, so you were willing to eat it.

Lisa, you worked so hard on your pizza, even though the recipe was non-existent, and you blamed yourself for its failure.

Michael, you are willing to take credit for a pizza that was a success to you by no effort of your own. You assume you could make a great pizza just because you've *had* a great pizza given to you.

None of these scenarios are realistic, but they are exactly how our team is approaching its work.

Working toward goals should be no different than working from a recipe. We should determine the food we want; find a recipe;

analyze the successes and failures of the recipe; and make the necessary changes to correct the process until we have successfully achieved the recipe.

We would never cook the way we did here, today. Let's choose to approach our work with the same intention we should use to approach our cooking by learning to SPEAR our goals."

Daniel's team enjoyed the pizza Daniel had already prepared for Michael's cooking.

"What is your takeaway?"

Write the one professional goal that is most important to you at this time in your life.

Write the one personal goal that is most important to you at this time in your life.

Journal about the pizza scenario. Do you see yourself in any of the characters of the scenario?

Confidence and adaptability are living, breathing attitudes. If not continuously fed, they will shrink to a point of futility.

Confidently,

DF

SPEAR: AN EXAMPLE

"If you can't explain what you do as a process, you don't know what you're doing"

~W. Edwards Deming

*T*he SPEAR:

SPEAR is the tool that can turn your goals into a recipe. SPEAR is an acronym for:

- Smart goal
- Plan
- Execution
- Analysis
- Realignment

S – Create a SMART (specific, measurable, achievable, realistic, time-bound) Goal.

P – Develop a PLAN of action; steps that will lead you toward your goal.

E – EXECUTE the plan.

A – ANALYZE the results of the plan; was it a success or a failure?

R – REALIGN the plan based on the successes you need to repeat and the failures from which you need to adapt. Notice that you are supposed to realign the plan and not the goal.

Example:

Day 1 -

SMART Goal – Make five calls a day every work day this week.

PLAN – Make calls in the half hour after lunch and before the afternoon meeting.

EXECUTE – On the first day, you make only two calls during the allotted time period.

ANALYZE – Success was the time to make the calls. Failure was the number of calls because you didn't take into account the amount of time to decide who to call.

REALIGN – Take ten minutes at the start of the day to jot down the five calls you plan to make.

(Your REALIGN becomes your PLAN.)

Day 2 -

EXECUTE – You make five calls, but didn't have any result from the calls.

ANALYZE – Success was making five calls. Failure was not having a call to action for the calls.

REALIGN – In addition to jotting down the call list, remember to tell the client about (a current promotion).

Day 3 –

EXECUTE – You make five calls, share news of an upcoming offering with each of them, and send more information about the offering to one of them.

ANALYZE – Successful calls, successful calls to action, and successful attainment of follow-up!

REALIGN – Repeat the process.

By the time you've hit **Days 4 and 5**, you are SPEARing on a new SMART Goal:

Using a list created each morning, make five calls each day to discuss our latest offering and ask permission to send a follow-up email with more information.

By applying the SPEAR to every task in your professional (and personal) life, you can begin to *crush* it in your day-to-day life and in your long-term goals. The more you SPEAR, the more habitual it will become. Soon, your intentional actions will be working toward greatness. The act of SPEARing is called, "SPEARITY."

The SPEARITY App
www.spearity.com

"What is your takeaway?"

Reflect on a goal you had in the past that you were unable to achieve but is still relevant today. Write down what that goal would have looked like if it were put into the SPEAR. In the ANALYZE portion of SPEAR, think about the reasons for which you failed and also think about the things that were successful.

Journal: Create a REALIGN for your past SMART goal!

SMART GOAL –

PLAN –

EXECUTE –

ANALYZE –

REALIGN –

The day you believe you're a Confident Enterpriser, you're not. You're more than likely an Overconfident Reciter who needs to be humbled.

Confidently,

DF

THE CONFIDENT ENTERPRISER™

"You must decide if you are going to rob the world or bless it with the rich, valuable, potent, untapped resources locked away within you."

~Myles Munroe

Daniel is good at multiple things and great at some things, but not all; he's the opposite of "Jack-of-all-Trades" opting to be the Master-of-Some. He did well in school, and probably better in College. Daniel has a good support and love system from his relationships and he recognizes it.

As a person who focuses on success, and focuses on failure, Daniel is living the life of a Confident Enterpriser.

The Risk Of Spiraling

A true Confident Enterpriser does not spiral. The Confident Enterpriser can begin to think he's successful because of just his own natural manner and that can turn into arrogance. When arrogance enters the picture, he or she will actually become an Overconfident Reciter, and that's where it's possible to tailspin. Occasionally, the Overconfident Reciter is struck with a difficult failure that takes out his or her confidence. Then, he or she becomes a Fearful Doer and can spiral from there.

The Confident Enterpriser is a hard place to hold, because confidence in and of itself is always a hair away from arrogance and cockiness. Because of the constant need to work to hold this quadrant, it is the "rented space" on the Confidence Quadrant. If the Confident Enterpriser continues in success while holding onto humility, though, it's something to appreciate. Consider what it would look like in the following individuals:

Athlete:

*Wants to work harder **and** smarter. The athlete works more at the THINGS that improve versus just mindless drilling. He or she will focus on the one area where performance is key,*

Entrepreneur:

He or she is a successful risk taker. They try new things to address new needs.

Service Person, Volunteer, or Cause-worker:

They lead other volunteers bringing them into passion for the cause

Parent:

They are encouraging their kids to pursue and take risks. They allow failure while also supporting successes.

Professional:

They are good at their jobs and open to professional development to get better.

As a Confident Enterpriser, you are where you want to be, but it's important to focus on what got you there and will keep you there. Here is how others may see a Confident Enterpriser:

Goals

- *Wants to succeed and is willing to work for it.*

Character Traits

- *Sees world from his or her perspective, alone*
- *Assumes everybody should have success*
- *Prone to fall into the Overconfident Enterpriser quadrant*

Endearing Qualities

- *Great with people*
- *Fun to be around*
- *Admired*

Connection to the Masses

- *We all have one or two times in life when we are prepared to win because we are prepared for what's coming. The Confident Enterpriser is the desired destination.*

Let's look back at our definitions:

Confidence *(TRUE Confidence)*–A feeling of success that is backed up, not just by a personal emotion, but also by measurable action.

Enterpriser – A willing risk-taker who embraces success and failure for constant improvement.

Awareness is the first step toward using The Confidence Quadrant. Look back at the Attitude Application assessment and review all of the "D" answers. As a Confident Enterpriser, in order to continue succeeding in that quadrant, you need to fight the Arrogance Monster day-to-day to prevent yourself from falling into Overconfident Reciter mode.

Your write-it-down and out-loud awareness statement is: *"I am aware that my success is a result of many moving parts, my own wins, AND the failures from which I've had to learn."*

By picking up this book, you are demonstrating an act of Confident Enterprising through a desire for professional and personal development toward BETTER . . . toward GREATNESS . . . toward CRUSHING IT.

1. Write a repeatable, daily affirmation statement that embraces your success.

2. Next, write a repeatable, daily promise to yourself about the areas in life you intend to improve upon on a routine basis.

"What is your takeaway?"

Reflect: Is there a time in your life when you were truly *crushing* it? Write about it, below.

Visualize! Journal below about what life as a Confident Enterpriser could mean for you.

A master is somebody that makes something look so easy a novice thinks they can do it.

~Confidently,

DF

RENTING THE SPACE

Practice isn't the thing you do once you're good. It's the thing you do that makes you good.

~Malcolm Gladwell

Who can be a Confident Enterpriser? The simple answer is everybody . . . and nobody. A famous anonymous quote tells us that we can't change our circumstances, but we can change our attitude. The Confidence Quadrant IS an Attitude Application, so it IS changeable! On the other hand, as we addressed when discussing Daniel, the Confident Enterpriser space is rented. As soon as a Confident Enterpriser holds the belief that he or she just "is" a natural success, without recognition of others or a personal need to seek continuous improvement, he or she has actually become and Overconfident Reciter.

There are some tools that can be used by potential "renters" to help them use success to gain confidence and failure to gain adaptability.

SUCCESS DECISION FLOW CHART

FAILURE DECISION FLOW CHART

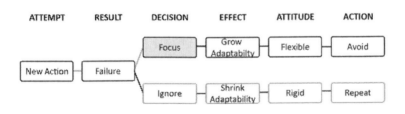

The Confidence Quadrant™

	IGNORE — FAILURE — FOCUS
FOCUS — SUCCESS	**OVERCONFIDENT RECITER™** Focus Success | Ignore Failure Confident | Rigid	**CONFIDENT ENTERPRISER™** Focus Success | Failure Confident | Flexible
SUCCESS — IGNORE	**AUTO REPEATER™** Ignore Success | Failure Timid | Rigid	**FEARFUL DOER™** Ignore Success | Focus Failure Timid | Flexible

FAILURE

IGNORE   FOCUS

1 – Continue *repeating* the same actions that led to successes in order to GROW CONFIDENCE.

What are some examples of successes you wish to continue repeating in *your* life?

2 – Avoid *repeating* the same actions that led to failures in order to GROW ADAPTABILITY.

What are some examples of failures you wish to avoid repeating in *your* life?

The humble leader will have difficulty kneeling before people because the people will continuously elevate the leader back above them.

Confidently,

DF

AFTER THE PIZZA

A bad system will beat a good person every time.

~W. Edwards Deming

Let's go back to Daniel's after the pizza . . .

Angela needs some hand-holding to build up some confidence and some gentleness in addressing her failures. Daniel creates a plan that sets regular, short meetings with Angela to encourage specific behaviors and actions that lead to success.

To encourage confidence, Daniel intentionally acknowledges gratitude to Angela for showing up to work, something that she had taken for granted as a success.

Daniel doesn't let failures go unnoticed, though. Angela failed to get an email out on time for a major client, because she had prioritized getting her reception area organized, something that Daniel had said was important. Daniel chose to sit down and create a list and priorities, for Angela. She learns to be adaptable, setting appropriate priorities and timelines to projects. Let's look at these changes in the form of the decision flow charts:

SUCCESS FLOW CHART:

ATTEMPT: Angela shows up to work on time.

RESULT: Success!

DECISION: With Daniel's help, Angela chooses to focus on the result. (Before the pizza, Angela would have chosen to ignore.)

EFFECT: Angela grows true confidence in knowing that she is dependable and reliable. (Ignoring would have led to shrinking confidence.)

ATTITUDE: Angela feels courageous in her professional life. (Ignoring would have led to timidity.)

ACTION: Angela continues repeating the action and continues the cycle of growing confidence. (Ignoring would have led to avoidance, or at least unintentional repetition of a positive action.

FAILURE FLOW CHART:

ATTEMPT: Prioritizing an important email.

RESULT: Failure.

DECISION: With Daniel's help, Angela chooses to focus on the result. (Before the pizza, Angela would have chosen to ignore.)

EFFECT: Angela's adaptability grows. (Before the pizza, ignoring would have led to shrinking adaptability.)

ATTITUDE: Angela becomes flexible. (Ignoring would have led to rigidity.)

ACTION: Angela avoids the same prioritization mistakes. (Ignoring would have had Angela repeating the same mistakes.)

You might notice that Daniel has to make some changes in this scenario, too. If Daniel wants to stay a confident enterpriser, he must also be working the SPEAR process! He makes changes, or, realignments, in how he is leading. He needs to make new (adapted) decisions to be better about clarity in objectives for Angela on the failure side, and intentional recognition on the success side.

Daniel must recognize the shortcomings of his own leadership and consistently work on his own professional development to ensure that his team chooses to follow him in confidence and adaptability.

Moving on to Lisa, Daniel needs to emphasize how, prior to Lisa's arrival, there was disarray. He comes up with a historical, comprehensive list of Lisa's successes that helped to improve the culture by limiting certain behaviors that seem like fun in the moment but ultimately lead to heartache and hurt feelings. All of those rules and policies that surround Lisa on her many posters were enacted out of chaos and Lisa brought in structure. The employee turnover virtually disappeared as a result of the improved, structured culture.

Daniel frequently encourages Lisa to embrace her successes. *"Fake it till you become it,"* is aligning the desired behavior with the physiological and mental mindset so that, over time, Lisa will become the confident person she needs to be to lead the accounting and finance department.

Using the flow chart examples from Angela's success and failure, what does Daniel's intentional leadership of Lisa look like?

SUCCESS FLOW CHART:

ATTEMPT:

RESULT:

DECISION:

EFFECT:

ATTITUDE:

ACTION:

FAILURE FLOW CHART:

ATTEMPT:

RESULT:

DECISION:

EFFECT:

ATTITUDE:

ACTION:

When it comes to Michael, Daniel needs to continue to encourage and praise Michael for his willingness to keep going at it and having the attitude to believe his sales will work themselves out.

That being said, Daniel needs to build relationship with Michael, in order to be able to address the fact that the sales are dipping. Daniel needs to constantly bring it back to the organization when addressing fails: "In order to meet the organization's goals..." If Daniel strikes at the confidence too much, Michael will go into tailspin. Michael needs to see his failures on a frequent basis, but with actionable, positive, confidence-building realignments. As he develops habits that grow his adaptability, those should also be praised to ensure he doesn't begin to shrink confidence.

Using the flow chart examples from Angela's success and failure, what does Daniel's intentional leadership of Michael look like?

SUCCESS FLOW CHART:

ATTEMPT:

RESULT:

DECISION:

EFFECT:

ATTITUDE:

ACTION:

FAILURE FLOW CHART:

ATTEMPT:

RESULT:

DECISION:

EFFECT:

ATTITUDE:

ACTION:

Using the flow chart examples from Angela's success and failure, what do the changes in Daniel's leadership look like?

SUCCESS FLOW CHART:

ATTEMPT:

RESULT:

DECISION:

EFFECT:

ATTITUDE:

ACTION:

FAILURE FLOW CHART:

ATTEMPT:

RESULT:

DECISION:

EFFECT:

ATTITUDE:

ACTION:

Darren Fisher

Greatness is something to which you must surrender . . . it doesn't submit to you.

Confidently,

DF

REALIGN

"I'm not going back, I'm moving ahead
here to declare to You my past is over..."
~Israel Houghton and Ricardo Sanchez

So, what are success and failure, really, and why do they matter?

My hope is that, as you have read this, you have been able to reflect on your strengths and weaknesses to see that everyone has them and everyone can overcome them, learn from them, and grow in confidence and adaptability through them. If we're not helping others and always amassing for ourselves, the satisfaction is limited and the impact is fleeting.

We tend to want everybody to be in a single quadrant together, where we can all relate and empathize with one another's attitude application. Instead, we're all struggling with different growths and spirals, while some try to move around and others are content where they are. Because of our differences, can people be tiring? Sure. Irritating? Of course. Antagonistic? Yes—and we can feel that way about ourselves, sometimes, too—but in the end we all need one another to collectively achieve greatness.

The tools provided in this book have been proven in practice with young and old, personal and professional, cross-industry and demographics. If they fail to work for you, let me know so that I may . . . realign.

In case you were wondering, I, too, use SPEARITY every day because I, too, want to rent the Confident Enterpriser quadrant.

Are you ready to be better?

Intentionally?

Maybe it's time for ***The Confidence Quadrant*** to be born in you.

Darren Fisher

Resources

Deming, W. Edwards. *The New Economics for Industry, Government, Education. Cambridge, MA: Massachusetts Institute of Technology, Center for Advanced Engineering Study, 1993. Print.*

Gladwell, Malcolm. *David and Goliath: Underdogs, Misfits, and the Art of Battling Giants. N.p.: n.p., n.d. Print.*

Pink, Daniel H. *Drive: The Surprising Truth about What Motivates Us. New York, NY: Riverhead, 2009. Print.*

Sinek, Simon. *Start with Why: How Great Leaders Inspire Everyone to Take Action. New York: Portfolio, 2009. Print.*

Darren Fisher

Acknowledgments

*Thank you to mom, Marva Bredendick, for her guidance, my father, Bob Fisher, for his entrepreneurial spirit, and my stepdad, Rob Bredendick, who introduced me to **"The New Economics."***

I'm intentionally grateful to those who knew me first and loved me best: Bryan Fisher, Katrina Fisher, Dawn Brackens, and Edward Fisher.

This book wouldn't exist without the life experiences of my family, especially my wife, Michele Fisher, my children Daryan and Daylen Fisher, and my stepdaughters, Carlyn and Kara Bickler. Thank you, also, to Ed and Sheila Helmke for treating me like a son.

For those who inspire me and hold me accountable to intentional betterment, I offer my gratitude, including: my lifelong friend, Shawn Collier, Maurice Jones, who reignited my love of reading, Joe DeRosa, for business advice and mentorship, and my Hill Point Church Family in River Hills, Wisconsin – specifically, my men's council, Doug Guffy, Pete Lillestolen, Mark Goodman, Larry Wilson, and James Ransom.

Thank you to all of the clients and teams I've been blessed to coach over the years as they have each helped to shape The Confidence Quadrant.

I offer my appreciation to those who made this book come to life, including editor, Stacy Marie Lewerenz, photographer, Stacy Kaat, designer, Katie Kimes-Lettau, publisher, Michael Nicloy, and the whole Reji Laberje Writing and Publishing team.

I'm grateful to the leadership team of Milwaukee Center for Independence – specifically, Annette Caraulia and Greg Bachrach, for believing in the SPEARITY process.

For continuing the intentional building of confidence and adaptability, I'm grateful to the SPEARITY application developer, Satwikeshwar "Satwik" Reddy P., the Darren Fisher Consulting advisory board of David Eurich, Jeff Killberg, Dan Meyer, and my "couster" (cousin-sister), Erika Tole, as well as my website developer, Latita Fisher.

Above all, I want to thank Jesus Christ, for the restoration he gave me when I was in a spiral . . . a tailspin. I am grateful to Him for LIFE and for life to the full. My Lord and Savior.

Darren Fisher

About the Authors

A successful entrepreneur, tech consultant, business coach, and—most importantly—Christian, husband, and father of four, Darren lives, works, and serves in the metropolitan Milwaukee area of his home. After the devastating losses of his first business and first marriage, Darren discovered a purpose in helping others to find their greatness. Today, he speaks, trains, coaches, and shares the value of SPEARity with those who are seeking to be better . . . intentionally. The proprietary tools he created for setting goals, personal and professional attitude development, and analyzing processes are helping thousands to crush it and now you can, too! Learn more at www.dfisherconsulting.com.

Working with Darren to create his book was Reji Laberje, Owner and Creative Director of Reji Laberje Writing and Publishing, where their vision is to use meaningful writing to, for, and from you to make far-reaching, positive impacts. Her books are being read by tens of thousands of readers and her company proudly stands behind bestsellers and storytellers, alike! Reji lives and serves in her community outside of Milwaukee, Wisconsin, alongside her full home of seven people and four pets. Learn more at www.rejilaberje.com.

Darren Fisher